Why Believe in God?

Basics of the Faith

Why Believe in God?

Daniel R. Hyde

P.O. BOX 817 • PHILLIPSBURG • NEW JERSEY 08865-0817

Page design by Tobias Design

Printed in the United States of America

Library of Congress Cataloging-in-Publication Data

Hyde, Daniel R.
  Why believe in God? / Daniel R. Hyde.
    p. cm. -- (Basics of the faith)
  Includes bibliographical references.
  ISBN 978-1-59638-212-1 (pbk.)
  1. God (Christianity) 2. Apologetics. I. Title.
BT103.H93 2011
231--dc22

2010054544

Ineffable is one of my favorite words in the English language. It comes from a Latin word, *ineffābilis*, which means something that is incapable of being adequately expressed in words. This eloquent adjective best describes my ineloquence when I have been asked time and time again why I believe in God. In my attempts to communicate an answer to this question either face to face or in written words to family, friends, and visitors to my congregation, I have most often felt that God's existence is ineffable and that my vain attempts were even more inadequate.

The reason for this inexpressibility is very simple: How do I explain or write down reasons for the most profound question in the universe? How can I, whom the Bible calls a creature that was made "of dust" (Gen. 2:7; cf. 3:19; Ps. 103:14), a "maggot" and a "worm" (Job 25:6), seek to present the case for the Creator of time, space, matter, and history? Furthermore, if the Bible compares the nations of the earth in relation to God as "a drop from a bucket" (Isa. 40:15), what does that make me? How do I try to explain what ultimately needs no explanation? Thus the word *ineffable* is fitting. Listen to Zophar, a friend of the ancient patriarch Job, express the ineffability of God:

> Can you find out the deep things of God?
> Can you find out the limit of the Almighty?

It is higher than heaven—what can you do?
  Deeper than Sheol—what can you know?
Its measure is longer than the earth
  and broader than the sea. (Job 11:7–9)

Ultimately, since God is ineffable, I should just "lay my hand on my mouth" and be quiet like Job did at the end of his story (Job 40:4). Nevertheless, in attempting to communicate to you an answer to this age-old question of why do we believe in God, I will whisper a few words between the fingers that are placed over my mouth, ever mindful of the apostle Paul's words:

Oh, the depth of the riches and wisdom and knowledge of God! How unsearchable are his judgments and how inscrutable his ways!

For who has known the mind of the Lord,
  or who has been his counselor?
Or who has given a gift to him
  that he might be repaid?"

For from him and through him and to him are all things. To him be glory forever. Amen. (Rom. 11:33–36)

FAITH SEEKING UNDERSTANDING

As we begin, let me first say a little about the limits of being able to "prove" God's existence. Traditionally, Christian theologians have offered several "proofs" for the existence of God. Among these proofs are the Ontological, Teleological, and Cosmological arguments. The *Ontological* argument basically says that because everything we can imagine as a most perfect being is limited by our conceptions, therefore a most perfect being must exist in reality. The *Teleological* argument basically says that since the universe looks and acts as if it were designed it must have a designer. The *Cosmological* argument basically says that everything that moves has to be moved by something else and that because this chain of movers cannot go on to infinity, there must be a first mover. In trying to understand or use these arguments it is vitally important for us to step back and remember that God is not an algebraic equation to be thought of in our minds or a substance merely to be experimented upon as in a petri dish. When we seek to answer the question of why we believe in God, we must keep before our minds and hearts the understanding that God is not simply a *what*, but a *he*, that is, God is a personal being who created us to have a relationship with him. The apostle Paul reminded the Christians in ancient Corinth of this fact when he taught them that if they were seeking to find God merely in an intellectual, logical, and philosophical way, they would never find him:

> For the word of the cross is folly to those who are perishing, but to us who are being saved it is the power of God. For it is written,

> I will destroy the wisdom of the wise,
>   and the discernment of the discerning I will thwart.

> Where is the one who is wise? Where is the scribe? Where is the debater of this age? Has not God made foolish the wisdom of the world? For since, in the wisdom of God, the world did not know God through wisdom, it pleased God through the folly of what we preach to save those who believe. For Jews demand signs and Greeks seek wisdom, but we preach Christ crucified, a stumbling block to Jews and folly to Gentiles, but to those who are called, both Jews

and Greeks, Christ the power of God and the wisdom of
God. For the foolishness of God is wiser than men, and the
weakness of God is stronger than men. (1 Cor. 1:18–25)

Our human wisdom is as foolishness to God, while what we see
as his foolish means of communicating himself in preaching is
really an exhibition of his wisdom and incomprehensible power.
So what can the traditional arguments above for God's existence
accomplish? Briefly, they serve a twofold purpose.

First and foremost, they are meant to assure the faith of
those who already believe in God. They do this because, as Christians, we believe in God in order to understand God. Faith seeks
understanding. This was how the ancient church father Augustine
(354–430) described the relationship between faith and understanding, when he said, "I believe, in order to understand; and I
understand, the better to believe."[1] As Christians, we believe in
God, but we must also seek to know him more and more over the
whole course of our lives. This is a part of what Jesus meant when
he said that a part of God's great commandment is to love God
with our minds (Matt. 22:37). The apostle Paul also prayed for
the church at Colossae to grow in their understanding of the God
in whom they believed, when he prayed, "We have not ceased to
pray for you, asking that you may be filled with the knowledge of
his will . . . increasing in the knowledge of God" (Col. 1:9–10).

Secondarily, presenting these proofs for the existence of
God certainly may be useful in witnessing to unbelievers. How-
ever, in doing so, our expectations should be limited. You see,
these proofs can only go as far as to show that our faith in God is
a reasonable faith, that it is not a blind leap in the dark. In using
these arguments we should not expect that in themselves they
can "prove" that God exists. As we will see below, we need to rely
upon the person and work of the Holy Spirit to convict unbeliev-

ers of their sin of unbelief, to convince them of God's existence, and to convert them to faith in God's Son, Jesus Christ.

Why do these arguments have limits? The reason is not because they are not true, but because we were all born sinners: "Behold, I was brought forth in iniquity, and in sin did my mother conceive me" (Ps. 51:5), the Psalmist confessed. And, Job asked, "What is man, that he can be pure? Or he who is born of a woman, that he can be righteous?" (Job 15:14). The apostle Paul listed some of the practical and damaging effects of this sin we are born with, which we call original sin, when he said those who do not believe or obey the one true God are "darkened in their understanding, alienated from the life of God because of the ignorance that is in them, due to their hardness of heart" (Eph. 4:18). Because of Adam's fall into sin, theologians from throughout Europe who gathered in Dordrecht in The Netherlands at the Synod of Dort in 1618–1619 said we are all characterized by "blindness of mind, horrible darkness, vanity, and perverseness of judgment . . . wicked, rebellious, and obdurate in heart and will, and impure in [all] his affections" (Canons of Dort, 3/4.1).[2] The Reformation theologian and pastor in Geneva, John Calvin (1509–1564), also recognized these effects when he wrote in response to critics of the Word of God in the sixteenth century: "Yet they who strive to build up firm faith in the Scripture through disputation are doing things backwards . . . the testimony of the Spirit is more excellent than all reason. For as God alone is a fit witness of himself in his Word, so also the Word will not find acceptance in men's hearts before it is sealed by the inward testimony of the Spirit."[3]

As Christians, then, we need to recognize that while it is true that the apostle Peter calls us to be "prepared to make a defense to anyone who asks you for a reason for the hope that is in you" (1 Peter 3:15) only God the Holy Spirit can change darkened understandings, ignorance, and hard hearts. Remarkably, this is exactly what the Lord said he would so graciously do to the Israelites thousands of years ago—and what he graciously continues to do today:

> I will sprinkle clean water on you, and you shall be clean from all your uncleannesses, and from all your idols I will cleanse you. And I will give you a new heart, and a new spirit I will put within you. And I will remove the heart of stone from your flesh and give you a heart of flesh. (Ezek. 36:25–26)

FOUR REASONS

So then, why do we believe in God? Here is one helpful outline:

> Q. How doth it appear that there is a God?
> A. The very light of nature in man, and the works of God, declare plainly that there is a God; but his word and Spirit only do sufficiently and effectually reveal him unto men for their salvation. (Westminster Larger Catechism, Q&A2)[4]

In this question and answer, three reasons are offered that our gracious God himself has set forth for sinful humanity: first, the light of conscience; second, the light of creation; and third, the light of the canon, that is, the Bible. I would also like to add to these three a fourth reason: the resurrection of Jesus Christ. This will be our outline for the rest of this booklet.

LIGHT OF CONSCIENCE

The first reason Christians believe in God is because the light of conscience testifies within us that he exists. The Larger Catechism calls this "the light of nature in man." What this means is that humans naturally know that God exists because God himself has implanted it into their conscience as his creation. The early church father from Palestine (modern-day Israel), Justin Martyr (100–165), called this innate knowledge the "seed of religion" (*semen religionis*) within us, and John Calvin called this innate knowledge of God in our minds the "sense of divinity" (*sensus divinitatis*). This light, seed, or sense in the conscience, heart, and mind is a part of what it means to be a human being.

Illustrated in the Bible

We see this light of conscience illustrated for us in the teaching of the Bible. For example, when the apostle Paul passed through the city of Athens in the first century and made his way up to the Areopagus, the place where the philosophers of the day gathered and debated, along the way he saw a long line of idols dedicated to every imaginable god. In fact, just in case the Athenians missed a god, they actually had an idol with this inscription: "To the unknown god" (Acts 17:23). The question is why would these great, reasonable philosophers of the ancient Graeco-Roman world create idols? The answer is that the light of their consciences testified that God was real and that he was watching them. As the Old Testament book of Ecclesiastes says, God has set eternity in the hearts of men (Eccl. 3:11).

Because of this light of conscience, Paul's words in Romans 1:18–32 take on greater meaning. The fact that people "suppress the truth" of God's existence (Rom. 1:18) and do everything to live as if he did not exist is evidence that the conscience encompasses a human knowledge of God. This is why Paul writes, "For although they knew God, they did not honor him as God or give thanks to him" (Rom. 1:21).

So why would people need to go to such lengths to deny God's existence, whether in words or deeds, if he did not exist? It is because he does exist that we sinfully seek to suppress this knowledge. Daily

God's existence is on our conscience, like bubbles rising up in our minds. Yet we frantically try to push each of these bubbles down to keep them from coming up and accusing our conscience. We heard the apostle Paul say we suppress this knowledge (Rom. 1:18, 21–23). Listen to how the Canons of the Synod of Dort express the knowledge of God in our consciences and the limits that it has.

> There remain, however, in man since the fall, the glimmerings of natural light, whereby he retains some knowledge of God, of natural things, and of the difference between good and evil, and discovers some regard for virtue, good order in society, and for maintaining an orderly external deportment. But so far is this light of nature from being sufficient to bring him to a saving knowledge of God, and to true conversion, that he is incapable of using it aright even in things natural and civil. Nay farther, this light, such as it is, man in various ways renders wholly polluted, and holds it [back] in unrighteousness; by doing which he becomes inexcusable before God. (3/4..4)[6]

Our sin nature does not want to acknowledge God because that would mean he is Lord over us and that our actions have consequences. Instead, we want to be God and do whatever pleases us. In fact, the Bible says those who think they are wise and try to suppress this knowledge from their minds are really "fools" (Ps. 14:1). A "fool" (Hebrew, *nabal*) in the Bible is not a person who doesn't have a brain or is not intelligent, but is a person who does not respond appropriately to the moral and religious sense that God has given them.

The light of our conscience, then, testifies to us that God exists. The reason we know he exists is simply because he is. One might object to this: "Well that's about as circular a reason as I have ever heard to prove God's existence." Yes it is, but I want you to answer the question how do you know *you* exist? You know you exist because you experience your body, your movements, your ups, your downs, and every aspect of your life. They are not illusions; they are not meaningless. You know you are because you are. We all know God exists, even after we have all had our understanding darkened (Eph. 4:18).

God is. The Bible begins with and assumes this truth when it says, "In the beginning God" (Gen. 1:1). This is why the great medieval theologian Anselm of Canterbury (1033–1109) "explained" God's existence with the aforementioned Ontological argument, saying, "We believe that You are something than which nothing greater can be thought."5 What Anselm was saying is similar to what the opening words of Scripture say, that is, we know God is because our minds are led upward, beyond all that we can think and contemplate. Why is this? Because all humans have been made in the image and likeness of God (Gen. 1:26–27); therefore all of us have this innate knowledge of God.

Illustrated in Thoughts and Actions

The light of conscience is also illustrated in our thoughts and actions. This innate knowledge that God exists is in fact the only thing that allows us to know anything else rightly. As the eloquent British philosopher and writer, C. S. Lewis (1898–1963), said, "I believe in Christianity as I believe that the Sun has risen: not only because I see it, but because by it I see everything else."7 What this means is that everything we think and do has an ultimate point of reference that gives meaning and purpose to this all.

For example, why can we say that the World War II leader of Germany, Adolf Hitler, was evil? Why were his actions against millions of Jews so morally repugnant? We can say this because evil is measured against the ultimate standard of God, who is morally good. Let me offer another example. Why exactly does 2+2=4? It does because God in his wisdom has ordered the universe with certain laws. Again, why am I as a husband able to love my wife? I can and must do so because God has eternally existed in love between Father, Son, and Holy Spirit. Why must you tell the truth to your interviewer when you go out looking for a job? You must because God is truth.

What all of this illustrates is that we cannot think rationally or live morally without presupposing or bearing witness to the existence of God. Again, the "fool" of Psalm 14 who denies God's existence is not foolish simply in a rational capacity, but a fool because his moral choices and actions lead to his eternal destruction. What this also means for us living in a multicultural global village is that reasoning as human beings and living ethically in community with one another was not invented as a cultural convention for us simply to get along with each other. Things like logic, laws, and ethics are not determined in a relative way by differing cultures with no absolute truth. In fact, saying there is no absolute truth and that all thinking and acting is relative is itself a statement of absolute truth. On the contrary, thinking coherently and living morally are based on the existence of God that we know in our consciences as we look at the world around us.

Struggling with Unbelief

Let me conclude this section on a pastoral note. In all that I have said so far, I want to acknowledge that this discussion is not just some rational and cognitive exercise. There is profound mystery when we speak of God and his existence. Remember, he is ineffable. There is utter transcendence when we seek to understand him and his ways. What this means even for us as Christians is that there is a tension between our knowledge of God's existence inherently and our struggle with that knowledge practically. We confidently know God is, but it is not always easy to believe or live accordingly. You know deep down inside that his existence is true, but it is not easy for you to believe when a loved one dies, when tragedy strikes a community, or when it seems impossible to make ends meet. I say this because we Christians are sinners too, although we often portray a holier-than-thou attitude or pretend we have it all figured out. Let me assure you that I do not.

One helpful passage of Scripture in dealing with doubt is found in the book of Hebrews, chapter 12. In this chapter the author to the Hebrews called his readers to "lay aside" what he called "*the* sin" which clings so closely to us (Heb. 12:1 KJV). He is not calling them to lay aside sin in general, but *the* sin that clings to us. What is this particular sin? The sin is unbelief. The writer speaks throughout his letter to the Hebrews of unbelief, particularly in 3:12–15 where he quotes David's words from Psalm 95: "Today, if you hear his voice, do not harden your hearts" (Ps. 95:7–8). The sin of unbelief "so easily beset[s] *us*," that is, Christians. Likewise, Calvin explained that as Christians we are perpetually and partially unbelievers: "For unbelief is so deeply rooted in our hearts, and we are so inclined to it, that not without hard struggle is each one able to persuade himself of what all confess with the mouth: namely, that God is faithful."[8] He went on to write,

> Surely, while we teach that faith ought to be certain and assured, we cannot imagine any certainty that is not tinged with doubt, or any assurance that is not assailed by some anxiety. On the other hand, we say that believers are in a perpetual conflict with their own unbelief.[9]

In our struggles we all must follow the example of the man who two thousand years ago brought his possessed son to Jesus to be healed. When he did this he prayed to the Lord, "I believe; help my unbelief" (Mark 9:24). This is why, as creatures made in the image of God, we simply need to acknowledge that we can think nothing greater than thoughts about him. After all, as the Creator himself asked Job, "Where were you when God created all things in the universe?" (Job chaps. 38–39).

LIGHT OF CREATION

The second reason we believe in God is because of the light of creation outside us testifying that he exists. God has not only implanted within us the internal testimony of our conscience, but he has also given us the external testimony of all the things his hands have made, like the beauty of a sunset, the majesty of a waterfall, or the tenderness of a snowflake.

The Testimony of David

For example, in Psalm 19 the Israelite king, David, describes the creation as a preacher, constantly proclaiming its Maker: "The heavens declare the glory of God, and the sky proclaims his handiwork. Day to day pours out speech, and night to night reveals knowledge" (Ps. 19:1–2). This proclamation of the glory and handiwork of God is universal to all peoples in all places of the human race. And David continues: "There is no speech, nor are there words, whose voice is not heard. Their voice goes out through all the earth, and their words to the end of the world" (Ps. 19:3–4). Of course like a preacher's words to a congregation, the proclamation of creation to all the inhabitants of the earth must be received by faith.

The Testimony of Paul

This light of creation is exactly what Paul proclaims in the aforementioned text in Romans 1. Here he teaches that God is knowable in creation: "For what can be known about God is plain to them, because God has shown it to them" (Rom. 1:19). He is plain or evident to us in the things we see above us, below us, and all around us. The early church father, Theophilus of Antioch (115–181), described this with the following analogy: "For as the soul in man is not seen, being invisible to men, but is perceived through the motion of the body, so God cannot indeed be seen by human eyes, but is beheld and perceived through His providence and works."[10] In beholding the things God has made, all humanity from creation onward has testified that he is the Creator and that everything that exists is his creation. In fact, Paul asserts the positive case for God's existence by stating the negative case of our suppression of his creation. In other words, the fact that humans create idols according to their own image is a testimony that the God who created the things represented by these idols exists. To ask it in the form of a question, where do humans get the idea to make an idol in the first place? This idea came from the knowledge God proclaims in the creation itself.

Every time we open our eyes we see the work of this Creator. What we learn about him in the work of his creation is that he is a *great and glorious* God: "The heavens declare the glory of God." The work of creation also testifies that he is a *skillful, creative, and ingenious* God: "the sky above proclaims his handiwork" (Ps. 19:1). When we look at the heavens and all the creation around us, their work teaches us that he is a *wise* God: "O LORD, how manifold are your works! In wisdom have you made them all; the earth is full of your creatures" (Ps. 104:24). Creation reveals that God is an *almighty* God because to create the vastness and the enormity of the universe, even as we know it, would take an infinite power beyond our imagination. In Paul's words, the work of God in creation shows us the "eternal power" of God (Rom. 1:20). Creation reveals that God is an *eternal* God because everything that came into being at some particular point in time was made by him who was already there: "Before the mountains were brought forth, or ever you had formed the earth and the world, from everlasting to everlasting you are God" (Ps. 90:2).

Our Response

Let me state, again, that this reason is no mere intellectual or mental exercise. God intends that the light of his creation should cause us to respond to him with faith and love for him. And how appropriate such a response is when we look upward and outward at creation. In recent years scientists have begun to publish research extending farther and farther into the known universe. We can view online the amazing pictures from the Hubble telescope in its Ultra Deep Field view photo. One photograph shows the deepest picture of space ever taken.[11] In it there are ten thousand galaxies. Sounds amazing, doesn't it? But then you learn that its perspective is like looking at a coin in front of you from seventy-four feet away, which means what exists in space is 12.7 million times more than can be seen by this photo. What should our response be to this? The light of creation should humble us in reverential awe and wonder, as the Psalmist poetically wrote.

> O LORD, our Lord,
>> how majestic is your name in all the earth!
> You have set your glory above the heavens.
> . . . .
> When I look at your heavens, the work of your fingers,
>> the moon and the stars, which you have set in place,
> what is man that you are mindful of him,
>> and the son of man that you care for him?
>> (Ps. 8:1, 3–4)

Another of the Psalms poetically describes how the light of creation should cause us to worship and praise God:

> Bless the LORD, O my soul!
>> O LORD my God, you are very great!
> . . . .
> May the glory of the LORD endure forever;
>> may the LORD rejoice in his works. (Ps. 104:1, 31)

Finally, the Psalms teach us that the light of creation should cause us to give thanks to God for his creative work. His creative work is also an expression of his love, and we have the privilege of enjoying it:

> Give thanks to the LORD, for he is good,
>   for his steadfast love endures forever.
> Give thanks to the God of gods,
>   for his steadfast love endures forever.
> Give thanks to the Lord of lords,
>   for his steadfast love endures forever;
> to him who alone does great wonders,
>   for his steadfast love endures forever;
> to him who by understanding made the heavens,
>   for his steadfast love endures forever;
> to him who spread out the earth above the waters,
>   for his steadfast love endures forever;
> to him who made the great lights,
>   for his steadfast love endures forever;
> the sun to rule over the day,
>   for his steadfast love endures forever;
> the moon and stars to rule over the night,
>   for his steadfast love endures forever. (Ps. 136:1–9)

You may respond, though, with the objection that we cannot verify there is a God or that he actually created everything. You may think that since there is no way to replicate the Creator or creation scientifically we will never know whether or not he exists, and therefore we can live in ignorant bliss or the suspended belief of agnosticism. Yet the Creator of the heavens and the earth himself expressed the foolishness of denying that the creation points to him as Creator. He did this when he rebuked Job. Thousands of years ago he answered Job, who was "the greatest of all the people of the east" (Job 1:3), out of a whirlwind,

> Who is this that darkens counsel by words without
> knowledge?
> Dress for action like a man;
> I will question you, and you make it known to me.

> Where were you when I laid the foundation of the earth?
> Tell me, if you have understanding.
> . . . .
> Can you bind the chains of the Pleiades
> or loose the cords of Orion?
> Can you lead forth the Mazzaroth in their season,
> or can you guide the Bear with its children?
> Do you know the ordinances of the heavens?
> Can you establish their rule on the earth?
> (Job 38:2–4, 31–33)

"Where were you when I laid the foundation of the earth?" (Job 38:4). What a humbling question. The answer to it is so obvious: I was nowhere because my existence depends upon God's will, power, and goodness. He is the Creator; I am the creature. He is the cause; I am the effect. And as the Old Testament prophets taught, God is like a potter, and we are merely the clay in his hands:

> But now, O LORD, you are our Father;
> we are the clay, and you are our potter;
> we are all the work of your hand. (Isa. 64:8)

> O house of Israel, can I not do with you as this potter has
> done? declares the LORD. Behold, like the clay in the potter's
> hand, so are you in my hand, O house of Israel. (Jer. 18:6)

LIGHT OF THE CANON

The third reason why we believe in God is because of the light of the canon, that is, the testimony that God has given in the Old and the New Testaments of his word. Recall the words of the aforementioned Larger Catechism, which says, "But his word and Spirit only do sufficiently and effectually reveal him unto men for their salvation." While conscience intimately from inside us and creation powerfully from outside us reveal God to all humans in a general way as the glorious, wise, eternal, and powerful Creator, historic Reformed Christianity teaches that only the Word of God can lead sinners to know God in the special way that gives a saving knowledge of him.

A Sufficient Light

Note well those two adjectives in the Catechism answer above: *sufficiently* and *effectually*. While conscience and creation reveal the existence of God, only the Word of God does so *sufficiently*. In Paul's words, that means the knowledge of God in creation is not able to lead us to salvation, but is only able to leave us "without excuse" (Rom. 1:20). Conscience and creation only testify that there is a God, that he has a claim on our lives, and that we are responsible to respond to him in faith and love. But in the Word we have all that we need for a saving knowledge of God. We learn in the Word that this God is not only a glorious, wise, eternal, and powerful Creator but that he is also a gracious, loving, and merciful Redeemer. We learn not only that he is Lord but also that he is Father; not only that he exists but also that he exists as three-in-one, as Father, Son, and Holy Spirit. The light of conscience and the light of creation are insufficient to do this.

An Effectual Light

And while conscience and creation reveal the existence of God, only the Word does so *effectually*. We see this again in the words of Psalm 19, where the Psalmist, David, compares and contrasts the knowledge of God in creation with the knowledge of God in the canon of his Word. While we saw above that the creation proclaims the glory and handiwork of God in a universal way to all peoples in all places (vv. 1–6), only the law, that is, the teaching of the LORD, can do the following:

> The law of the LORD is perfect,
>> reviving the soul;
> the testimony of the LORD is sure,
>> making wise the simple;
> the precepts of the LORD are right,
>> rejoicing the heart;
> the commandment of the LORD is pure,
>> enlightening the eyes;
> the fear of the LORD is clean,
>> enduring forever;
> the rules of the LORD are true,
>> and righteous altogether.
> More to be desired are they than gold,
>> even much fine gold;
> sweeter also than honey
>> and drippings of the honeycomb.
> Moreover, by them is your servant warned;
>> in keeping them there is great reward. (Ps. 19:7–11)

One of the great confessions of faith of the Protestant Reformation, the Belgic Confession (1561), reflects upon what Psalm 19 and Romans 1 teach concerning the comparison and contrast between creation and the canon.

> We know him by two means: first, by the creation, preservation, and government of the universe; which is before our eyes as a most elegant book, wherein all creatures, great

and small, are as so many characters leading us to contemplate *the invisible things of God*, namely, *his eternal power and Godhead*, as the Apostle Paul saith (Rom. i. 20). All which things are sufficient to convince men, and leave them without excuse. Secondly, he makes himself more clearly and fully known to us by his holy and divine Word; that is to say, as far as is necessary for us to know in this life, to his glory and our salvation. (art. 2)[12]

This confession of faith goes on to say that the canon of Scripture is rooted in "a special care which [God] has for us and our salvation" (art. 3). God gave the Bible because he is concerned for our souls and their salvation from sin. As the ancient church father from Carthage in North Africa, Tertullian (160–220), explained,

> But that we might approach more fully and impressively both to Himself and His ordinances and will, He gave in addition the document of Scripture, in case any one should wish to enquire about God, and having enquired, to find Him, and having found, to believe, in Him, and having believed, to serve Him . . . He who hears them will find God; and he who is at pains to understand them will also be compelled to believe.[13]

The Character of Scripture

Why do we say the Bible is able to bring us to a saving knowledge of God? After all, isn't it just another book, or at best, the religious feelings of some people in a far off time and place? Also, there are many competing holy books among the religions of the world. Judaism has the *Tanach*—the Law, the Prophets, and the writings of the Old Testament; Islam has the *Qur'an* (and the *Hadith* for Sunni Muslims); Hinduism has the *Bhagavad Gita*, the *Upanishads*, and the *Vedas*; Taoism has the *Tao-te-ching*; and Confucianism has *The Analects*.

Even among Christians there is no consensus as to which books make up the Word of God. Both the Roman Catholic and the Eastern Orthodox Churches recognize the Old and New Testaments along with what is called the Apocrypha (e.g., Tobit, Judith, Wisdom, Jesus Sirach, Baruch, and 1–2 Maccabees). These books were named *apocrypha*, which comes from the Greek word *apokruphos*, meaning "hidden," because their origin and authorship were unknown.

On the other hand, confessional Protestants such as Reformed, Anglican, and Lutheran churches recognize only the Old and New Testaments as the Word of God. While it is true that many writings claim to be the will of God for humankind, the difference is that the Bible not only attributes this for itself but also evidences this claim. In a word, the Bible has a different character than any other holy book in the world. It not only says it is the inspired, infallible, and authoritative Word of God, but it proves itself to be what it says it is.

The Bible witnesses to itself that it is the *inspired* Word of God. Inspiration does not mean that God literally dictated his Word to the prophets and apostles, or that they were religiously moved and inspired to write their feelings down for us, but that since God has "breathed out" his Word using the individual gifts and abilities of the writers, that it is holy and sacred (2 Tim. 3:16). Listen to how the Bible speaks of itself:

Long ago, at many times and in many ways, God spoke to our fathers by the prophets, but in these last days he has spoken to us by his Son. (Heb. 1:1–2)

Knowing this first of all, that no prophecy of Scripture comes from someone's own interpretation. For no prophecy was ever produced by the will of man, but men spoke from God as they were carried along by the Holy Spirit. (2 Peter 1:20–21)

And how from childhood you have been acquainted with the sacred writings, which are able to make you wise for salvation through faith in Christ Jesus. All Scripture is breathed out by God and profitable for teaching, for reproof, for correction, and for training in righteousness, that the man of God may be competent, equipped for every good work. (2 Tim. 3:15–17)

The Bible also claims itself to be the *infallible* Word of God. This means that the Word of God is true in all that it teaches, and it cannot lead us into error in what it teaches. Consider these words from the Bible:

The words of the LORD are pure words,
    like silver refined in a furnace on the ground,
    purified seven times. (Ps. 12:6)

Every word of God proves true;
    he is a shield to those who take refuge in him. (Prov. 30:5)

Finally, the Bible claims for itself that it is the *authoritative* Word of God. Because they are inspired and infallible, the books that make up the Bible are our only and ultimate source and foundation of theology and practice, doctrine and life. As Peter exults, "His divine power has granted to us all things that pertain to life and godliness, through the knowledge of him who called us to his own glory and excellence, by which he has granted to us his precious and very great promises" (2 Peter 1:3–4). We see this authority, for example, in the numerous Old Testament passages that begin by saying, "Thus says the Lord" (e.g., Isa. 7:7) and in New Testament passages such as our Lord Jesus Christ's words: "You have heard that it was said to those of old, 'You shall not murder; and whoever murders will be liable to judgment.' But I say to you . . ." (Matt. 5:21). We also see this authority

in passages such as the one in Revelation, where Jesus warns us not
to add to or subtract from his Word.

> I warn everyone who hears the words of the prophecy of
> this book: if anyone adds to them, God will add to him
> the plagues described in this book, and if anyone takes
> away from the words of the book of this prophecy, God
> will take away his share in the tree of life and in the holy
> city, which are described in this book. (Rev. 22:18–19)

The Work of the Spirit

Claiming that the Bible is the only sufficient and effectual
means of coming to a saving knowledge of God is a weighty claim.
This begs the question of how mere words of ink written on paper
can convince anyone that there is a God. The answer lies in the fact
that it is not just the bare words of ink on paper that do this. Mere
paper and ink cannot change us. After all, not everyone who reads
the pages of a Bible is convinced of God's existence or necessarily
converted to faith in his Son, Jesus Christ. Paul illustrated this sad
reality in the first century by those who heard the Old Testament
read week by week in synagogues, yet did not believe that Jesus of
Nazareth was their Messiah and Savior.

> For to this day, when they read the old covenant [Old Tes-
> tament], that same veil remains unlifted, because only
> through Christ is it taken away. Yes, to this day whenever
> Moses [Genesis–Deuteronomy] is read a veil lies over
> their hearts. But when one turns to the Lord, the veil is
> removed. Now the Lord is the Spirit, and where the Spirit
> of the Lord is, there is freedom. (2 Cor. 3:14–17)

What this means is that it is not only the Word itself, but the
Word joined together with the Holy Spirit that can bring us to a

sufficient and effectually saving knowledge of the one true God. The Spirit of Christ alone can take away the veil that lies over our eyes. Lest we think Paul was accusing the Jews of something he had no knowledge or experience of, let me remind you that Paul was known as Saul of Tarsus before he was converted to Christ. As Saul he was known as an extremely zealous rabbi of the Jewish people who persecuted Christians. As recorded in the book of Acts, the history of the early church, "Saul was ravaging the church, and entering house after house, he dragged off men and women and committed them to prison" (Acts 8:3). Paul later described himself before his conversion in this way: "If anyone else thinks he has reason for confidence in the flesh, I have more: circumcised on the eighth day, of the people of Israel, of the tribe of Benjamin, a Hebrew of Hebrews; as to the law, a Pharisee; as to zeal, a persecutor of the church; as to righteousness under the law, blameless" (Phil. 3:4–6). As the example of Paul illustrates, it took the powerful work of God the Holy Spirit to save him from his wicked and error-driven ways and to open his eyes to understand the claims of the Word of God concerning Jesus (Acts 9:1–19).

In theological terms, this means that while the Word of God is the instrumental cause of salvation, that is, the means by which the Lord brings us to faith, it is the Holy Spirit who is the efficient cause, that is, the power that actually accomplishes the work. As an example of this we can look at what Paul says in 1 Corinthians 2. Here Paul says that when he came to the church of the Corinthians, he "did not come proclaiming . . . the testimony of God with lofty speech or wisdom," but instead his "speech and . . . message were not in plausible words of wisdom, but in demonstration of the Spirit and of power" (1 Cor. 2:2, 4). The purpose of this was "that your faith might not rest in the wisdom of men but in the power of God" (1 Cor. 2:5). What Paul proclaimed was not understood by "the rulers of this age" (1 Cor. 2:8), but "these things God has revealed to us through the Spirit" (1 Cor. 2:10).

The reason for this distinction is found in this fact: "The natural person does not accept the things of the Spirit of God, for they are folly to him, and he is not able to understand them because they are spiritually discerned" (1 Cor. 2:14). The Holy Spirit alone can and must remove the veil from our eyes.

THE RESURRECTION OF JESUS CHRIST

Philosophers and theologians have debated the existence of God and the proofs of his existence from conscience, creation, and the canon for centuries, as have ordinary believers and nonbelievers—and the debate still rages. Yet the ultimate reason that these arguments have any power to persuade from belief to unbelief is because Jesus Christ was raised from the dead after he was crucified. As Christians say in the Easter Liturgy, "Alleluia! Christ is Risen! The Lord is risen indeed! Alleluia!" (Mark 16:6; Luke 24:34).

Because we as humanity have been suppressing the knowledge of God ever since Adam and Eve sinned in the Garden of Eden (Gen. 3), God himself had to act dramatically in order to save us from our foolishness. He did this by sending his very own eternal Son to become man: "For God so loved the world, that he gave his only Son, that whoever believes in him should not perish but have eternal life" (John 3:16). Theologians call the coming of the Son of God into the world the "incarnation" because in this act the Son of God became a man. As the apostle John says, "And the Word became flesh and dwelt among us" (John 1:14). The Son of God became visible, tangible, and physical. John, the disciple "whom Jesus loved" (John 13:23), describes the reality and the earthiness of this eternal Word made flesh. "That . . . which we have heard, which we have seen with our eyes, which we have looked upon and have touched with our hands" (1 John 1:1).

After this eternal Son of God became a man, he walked the earth for approximately thirty-three years. He then was "crucified, dead, and buried," as the Apostles' Creed states. "But now is Christ risen from the dead" (1 Cor. 15:20 KJV). In his great chapter on the resurrection in 1 Corinthians 15, the apostle Paul teaches us that the resurrection of Jesus Christ was the culmination of our salvation. Elsewhere he argues that the resurrection testifies to the truthfulness of all that Jesus said and did, and that by the resurrection God the Father "declared [him] to be the Son of God in power" (Rom. 1:4). Listen to how the apostle teaches the vital significance of the resurrection to Christian faith and life:

> And if Christ has not been raised, then our preaching is in vain and your faith is in vain. We are even found to be misrepresenting God, because we testified about God that he raised Christ, whom he did not raise if it is true that the dead are not raised. For if the dead are not raised, not even Christ has been raised. And if Christ has not been raised, your faith is futile and you are still in your sins. Then those also who have fallen asleep in Christ have perished. If in Christ we have hope in this life only, we are of all people most to be pitied. (1 Cor. 15:14–19)

The resurrection of Jesus is vital in another way as well. It has always fascinated me that the apostle Paul, in reasoning with the great philosophers of his day about the existence and nature of God on Mars Hill in Acts 17, did not point these philosophers to Christ's death, or to life's purpose, or to God's love for the sinner, or to God's "wonderful plan for their lives"—as is so often done today by Christian evangelists. Instead, the apostle Paul, who saw the resurrected Christ on the road to Damascus, pointed the philosophers to the *resurrection* of Jesus Christ:

> The times of ignorance God overlooked, but now he
> commands all people everywhere to repent, because
> he has fixed a day on which he will judge the world in
> righteousness by a man whom he has appointed; and of
> this he has given assurance to all by raising him [Jesus
> Christ] from the dead. (Acts 17:30–31)

Paul's greatest "defense" of the Christian faith to the learned
philosophers of the ancient world was actually to proclaim the resurrection of Jesus. This historical fact was the basis of everything
he preached. It is also the basis of everything we believe.

> Now I would remind you, brothers, of the gospel I
> preached to you, which you received, in which you stand,
> and by which you are being saved . . . For I delivered to
> you as of first importance what I also received: that Christ
> died for our sins in accordance with the Scriptures, that
> he was buried, that he was raised on the third day in
> accordance with the Scriptures. (1 Cor. 15:1–2, 3–4)

CONCLUSION: GOD *IS*

You may be reading this booklet because you are interested
in finding and coming to know the God who made you. This *is*
your highest purpose. As A. W. Tozer (1897–1963) once wrote,
"Without doubt, the mightiest thought the mind can entertain
is the thought of God, and the weightiest word in any language
is its word for God."[14] As we have seen, God testifies of his own
existence in the light of conscience he placed within us, in the
light of creation he placed above, below, and around us, and in the
light of the canon of Scripture that he has given to sufficiently and
effectually lead us to a relationship with him. And as we just saw,
if you want to find God, the greatest proof of all is to look into the

empty tomb outside of the city gates of Jerusalem. Yet you need to look not with the eyes of the body, but with the eye of the soul, that is, with faith. When you do so you will find that because the tomb is still empty, God *is*.

Why believe in God, then? I believe in God because there is a light within my conscience that testifies of his existence. I believe in God because there is light in the creation pointing me to him. I believe in God because the light of the canon of Scripture shines upon him. And I believe in God, most importantly of all, because the tomb of Jesus Christ is empty. Let me conclude with an account from the life of Job. After Job spent many sleepless nights and untold amounts of energy questioning God as to whether he was good and just, God summoned Job to appear before him. The book of Job describes this encounter as if it were in a courtroom. In this climactic scene God interrogated Job. The Lord concluded his trial of Job's arrogant disbelief by saying, "Shall a faultfinder contend with the Almighty? He who argues with God, let him answer it" (Job 40:2). What God was saying to Job, and what he is saying to you, is to stop contending with God. You need to stop suppressing the knowledge of him that you feel in your heart, see with your eyes, and hear with your ears. You need to stop running from him in your mind with your arguments against him and stop denying him by living a life as if he did not exist. Instead, you need to recognize what you know to be true in your conscience. You need to recognize what you see with your eyes in creation. You need to recognize what you hear in his Word. And with this knowledge, you need to fall on your knees and confess your innumerable sins before Almighty God. But in your confession, do not simply come before God as Creator and Judge, as the One greater than yourself, but come to him in faith as your heavenly Father. This is possible through believing in his resurrected Son, Jesus Christ. You see, God does not desire to condemn you, but to save you from your sins, from yourself, and from his own just wrath. This is why he says to you now:

Fear not, I am the first and the last, and the living one. I died, and behold I am alive forevermore, and I have the keys of Death and Hades. (Rev. 1:17–18)

And this is eternal life, that they know you the only true God, and Jesus Christ whom you have sent. (John 17:3)

NOTES

1. Cited in *Catechism of the Catholic Church* (New York: Image/Doubleday, 1995), 49.
2. Philip Schaff, ed., David S. Schaff, rev., *The Creeds of Christendom*, 3 vols. (1877; repr., Grand Rapids: Baker, 1996), 3:588.
3. John Calvin, *Institutes of the Christian Religion*, ed. John T. McNeill, trans. Ford Lewis Battles, The Library of Christian Classics, vols. 20–21 (Philadelphia: The Westminster Press, 1960), 1.7.4.
4. *Westminster Confession of Faith* (1958; repr., Glasgow, Scotland: Free Presbyterian Publications, 2009), 129.
5. *Proslogion*, 2, in *Anselm of Canterbury: The Major Works*, ed. Brian Davies and G. R. Evans (Oxford, England: Oxford University Press, 1998), 87.
6. Schaff, *The Creeds of Christendom*, 3:588.
7. C. S. Lewis, *The Weight of Glory* (New York: HarperCollins Publishers, 1976), 140.
8. Calvin, *Institutes*, 3.2.15.
9. Calvin, *Institutes*, 3.2.17.
10. Theophilus to Autolycus, 1.5, in *Ante-Nicene Fathers: Volume 2*, ed. Alexander Roberts and James Donaldson (1885; repr., Peabody, Mass.: Hendrickson Publishers, 2004), 90.
11. http://hubblesite.org.
12. Schaff, *The Creeds of Christendom*, 3:384.
13. *Apologeticus*, 18; *The Apology of Tertullian for the Christians*, trans. T. Herbert Bindley (Oxford, England: Parker and Co., 1890), 57, 59.
14. A. W. Tozer, *The Knowledge of the Holy* (1961; repr., New York: Harper Collins Publishers, 1992), 2.